WHEN YOUR FRIEND IS DYING

Elizabeth Dean Burnham

Published by

√Chosen Books, Lincoln, Virginia 22078
of the Zondervan Corporation
Grand Rapids, Michigan 49506

Dedication

to

Peter J. Mozden, M.D.
F.A.C.S.

and his medical staff team of fellows,
residents, interns, and nurses at University Hospital,
Boston, and to all medical professionals dedicated to the
eradication of cancer

and to

Monty, Suzanne, and Marybeth,
and to all who loved and supported me as I lived
amidst my dying

and for

all who long to care for loved ones who are ill.

Library of Congress Cataloging in Publication Data

Burnham, Elizabeth Dean.
 When your friend is dying

  1. Ovaries—Cancer—Patients—Massachusetts—Biography.
2. Christian life—1960. 3. Burnham, Elizabeth Dean. I. Title.

RC280.08B87   1982   248.8'6   82-17725
ISBN 0-310-60341-2

WHEN YOUR FRIEND IS DYING
Copyright © 1982 Elizabeth Dean Burnham

Printed in the United States of America.

Chosen Books, a division of the Zondervan Corporation, Grand Rapids, Michigan 49506. Editorial offices for Chosen Books are in Lincoln, Virginia 22078.

ISBN 0-310-60341-2

Unless otherwise indicated, the Bible translation quoted in this book is the New International Version, © 1978 by New York International Bible Society; published by The Zondervan Corporation, Grand Rapids, MI 49506.

Contents

Introduction

"I don't care if I never make a cent from this book. I just want it to help people."

I heard these words recently in conversation with Betsy Burnham, and now her wish is becoming reality. Through our friendship, and now through this book, I have been helped by Betsy's practical wisdom.

How many times have I heard the dreaded news that a dear and cherished friend has cancer or some other life-threatening disease? And in words—or in "sighs too deep for words," as St. Paul puts it—my heart has cried: "Lord, how can I help?" Sometimes I've felt awkward, unsure, even fearful that in reaching out I might be insensitive or clumsy, hurting the one I wanted so much to help. And so my prayer continued: "Lord, teach me. What kind of help is truly helpful?"

Betsy's book is an answer to that prayer. If you share my feelings of inadequacy when illness strikes someone close to your heart, *When Your Friend Is Dying* will be a valuable resource for you as it was for me. According to Betsy's wish and design, this is a practical book. Yet it is not just a "how-to" manual.

Throughout, you will see glimpses of Betsy's own journey, her personal struggle with a devastating illness. I cried in parts, not because this is a sad book—it isn't. But with characteristic honesty, my friend shares the emotional and physical pain that has plagued her since she began her valiant struggle for life. On every page, I see etched the beauty of her character and person. I sense her commitment to her husband, Monty, and their daughters, Suzanne and Marybeth. And I feel the love that permeates their life together. She ached, and I ached—and unbidden, the tears fell.

Yet there is the strength of hope in these pages. The integrity of Betsy's faith is intact from start to finish. I believe that, as she wrote this book, she was wrapped in God. She yielded her experience to Him—from the height of her hope to the depth of her anger and despair—and I believe He will bring from it beauty, strength, and help for others.

When Your Friend Is Dying is a much-needed book, and I'm eager to share it with friends, and to place copies in our church library. And I know it will pass from hand to hand to hand.

I am delighted to commend to you this gold mine of practical help!

Colleen Townsend Evans
Washington, D.C.

Foreword

Soon after I was diagnosed as having cancer, I was introduced to a woman from a neighboring church who had heard about my illness. After a smile and a handshake, she asked me, "How does a person like me help someone with a malignancy?"

Her question was wonderfully direct, with no pretense. It said: "I want to understand your emotional, physical and spiritual needs."

I thought long and hard about her question. In trying to answer her—and other concerned, caring people like her—I found myself writing this book.

Cancer and other life-threatening illnesses know no boundaries.* We are all vulnerable to the sudden onslaught of sickness. Unexpectedly, a husband, wife, child, neighbor or friend is stricken, and I've heard the question echoed many times: "How does a person like me help?"

Throughout my own long battle for life, I've gradually learned how I can be a more caring friend to others who are ill.

---

* Cancer alone has a devastating effect on the population. According to the American Cancer Society, "Almost 56 million Americans now living will eventually have cancer; one in four according to present rates. Over the years, cancer will strike in approximately two of three families. In the '70s,

There are many people who have helped me—and many others who might have helped, with a little bit of encouragement and foresight.

Sickness is not comfortable for anyone. Faced with the realities of life, you may learn some things about yourself that are humbling or embarrassing. You may discover in yourself a lack of sensitivity, a desire to pull away from a friend in need. Or you may find a real desire to help—but a lack of practical know-how.

In these pages, I have tried to present the most useful, practical suggestions for helping, reaching out and touching in a significant way the life of a friend who is suffering with a life-threatening illness.

Betsy Burnham
January 1982

there were an estimated 3.5 million cancer deaths, over 6.5 million new cancer cases and more than 10 million people under medical care for cancer" (American Cancer Society, 1981 Facts and Figures, American Cancer Society, Inc., New York, N.Y. p. 3).

I

Seeing the Need

The stitches in my huge abdominal incision pulled uncomfortably as I shifted position to look out the window. I was grateful to be even this close to the outdoors. Splotches of warm, filtered sunshine played on the sill and on the sterile bedclothes at my feet. Though the tall, dreary buildings of Boston obstructed much of my view of the adjacent park and its budding trees, I knew that spring was abroad. On the street below, I could see nurses and orderlies lingering coatless in conversation.

Glancing over at my roommate's bed, I could see that she was resting quietly. Barbara was 42 years old, and suffering with advanced cancer. Now her dark hair was spread over the pillow and her eyes were closed.

A movement in the doorway caught my eye. Two stylishly dressed women peered in cautiously as if they feared they were in the wrong place. Seeing Barbara, they looked relieved.

"Is she awake?" the short plump one whispered hoarsely as she tiptoed toward the bed. Barbara's eyes fluttered open.

"Hi, Barbara!" Their cheery greeting was cut short as they moved closer and got a better look at their friend.

"Helen, Marie. How nice of you to come and see me," Barbara murmured, brushing the hair away from her face. She fumbled weakly for the electronic bed control, trying to raise herself to a sitting position. Her face was drawn, thin,

11

and her skin was a light gray.

As she adjusted herself, the two friends stood uncertainly at the foot of her bed. Marie, the taller woman in the yellow suit, held a cone of green florist's paper tightly in one hand. I could tell by their nervous smiles and sideways glances that they were struggling with what to say next.

"You look marvelous," Marie blurted out, clutching her flowers.

I winced inwardly. The incongruity of the scene amazed me. No one could look at Barbara, a wasted, pathetic woman, and say she looked "marvelous." And yet I could feel the struggle these friends were going through. They so wanted to be positive and hopeful in the face of Barbara's grave illness.

Quickly Helen spoke up, aiming for a less threatening subject.

"What a nice room," she quipped and, finding herself up a blind alley, tried again. "When I was in for my hysterectomy, I felt just as you do now—sore and tired. They gave me pain pills for as long as I needed them, but I'll tell you, the first few days were rough. Then you kind of gradually get back on your feet again. Before you know it, you won't even need help to get around. But you might be bent over for a while," she added with a little laugh.

"And did I ever tell you about the medical student who tried to take my stitches out?" she continued. Barbara smiled slightly, shaking her head, but Helen was already into the story.

"Well, I'll tell you, it was awful. He'd never removed stitches before as far as I could tell. He kept cutting me instead of the stitches. Whew! I needed a sedative when that was all over."

As she spoke, I was baffled. Barbara wasn't in the hospital for an operation. She was having a long series of radiation treatments in a desperate attempt to arrest her spreading disease. So why was Helen going on and on about surgery?

The plumpish woman was still talking. "Pretty soon the day will come, and you'll go home. You can't believe how good it feels to get out of here. I was so excited when they let me out. Of course, you'll have to be a good patient at home. You'll just have to let us come over and wait on you."

I looked at Barbara with her deep-set, dark eyes, and wondered if she would ever go home again.

"Where can I get a vase for these flowers?" Marie spoke up again, having recovered a bit from her awkward entrance.

Barbara raised herself up on one elbow, and reached over to the bedside table. Pushing aside pictures, glasses, and other bouquets, she lifted up a dried-up arrangement. "You can throw these out," she suggested, "and get some fresh water from the bathroom."

Marie relaxed a little with something to do. She disappeared into the bathroom to arrange her roses.

"What a lovely day it is outside!" Helen slipped off her chic spring blazer, and settled herself into the leather easy chair at Barbara's side.

"It's finally acting like spring," she continued. "Everything is about to bloom. In fact, you should see the forsythia in my yard. I do love this time of year."

Marie returned, with her roses settled in the vase, and perched on the end of Barbara's bed.

"You know, Barb, we thought of you all during lunch," she joined in. "We had your favorite—fresh crab salad. If you'll just hurry up and get well, we'll take you out for a special treat. How does that sound?"

Helen took over again. "I guess mid-afternoon wasn't the best time to drive through the city. We had such a time finding this hospital. I know where everything is in down-town Boston, but I never come here to the South End. I made a couple wrong turns, and we got stuck on a street where they were tearing up the pavement. And I thought we'd never find a parking place," she finished, rolling her eyes.

"I'm sorry you had such a hard time getting to see me. Thanks for going to so much trouble," Barbara said softly. "These roses are so lovely. Roses are my favorite."

From where I lay, I could see that Barbara's eyes were drooping and that she had slumped down into her pillows. Most afternoons, she slept a great deal. But I knew she wanted to be polite to her friends.

"How are things at home—at the church?" she asked.

"Fine. Just fine," Marie reassured her from the foot of the bed.

"Things are moving ahead," Helen took over. "We had a women's tea for new members and it went beautifully. We missed that special nut bread you always bake, though."

"The pastor gave a fine sermon on Easter Sunday," Marie chimed in again. "He talked about spring and new life. And lots of new people were there. It was exciting and . . ."

Barbara was valiantly fighting off sleep now. She inter-rupted apologetically.

"I hate to be such a party pooper, girls," she said, not without some effort. "But I get so tired. And the pain takes over. I'm going to buzz the nurse for a pain pill, and I'll have to sleep."

As she turned to reach for the buzzer, Helen and Marie glanced at each other. I saw the frozen, frightened look in their eyes. The smiles were gone. I knew that, for the first time, they had realized the seriousness of their friend's condition—her weakness, her pain, her *cancer.*

"Ah, of course, dear," Helen patted her arm sympathetically. "Come on, Marie. We've spent too much time with Barbara already. She's tired out."

Again, I was bewildered at their superficial response.

Barbara's in so much pain, and they don't even acknowledge it, I thought. *If only they would ask her where it hurts—or how she's handling all this emotionally.*

The two women had gathered up their blazers and handbags and were already slipping out the door. Helen turned and gave a final cheery wave. Then they were gone.

A nurse came in and drew the curtain around Barbara's bed. I watched the IV bottle drip-dripping into the tube that was injected into my own neck. The sunlight had crept a little further up the bedclothes, but my thoughts remained with the two retreating visitors.

I tried to imagine them at that moment, standing in the corridor, perhaps, waiting for the elevator. I could even feel the mixture of emotions—relief at being away from the sickroom, pity, a choking kind of sorrow, helpless frustration. Probably they said very little. Maybe their eyes were shining with tears.

Then the questions began rolling through my mind.

It was great, I conceded, that Barbara's friends made the effort to come. But why were they so unable to help carry her load? Why was their visit so tiring and not refreshing? Sure, it's difficult to put yourself in the place of someone who's lying in a hospital bed. But is it impossible to really "get with" someone who's suffering?

The questions reached a deeper level. Had these friends *truly* come to help Barbara? Or was it only out of obligation? The outward evidence was sad.

They had let her know, perhaps unwittingly, that the trip was a bother. They had talked about delicious food and good weather that she was too sick to enjoy. They chatted about

happenings at home from which she was far removed. Never
once did they talk directly about *her*—about her illness, her
treatments, her family, her feelings.

No, they really did care about Barbara, I decided. The
flowers, the smiles, the chatter—it was all meant to help.
They, like most people, meant well. Still, there was a wide gap
between their intentions and their ability to reach out and
help.

And more than that, these ladies had come representing
a church. As a pastor's wife, I felt sad to realize how little the
church has done to train its people in sensitivity to suffering
and need. Most of us are so afraid to touch real hurt, so
ill-prepared to face real anxiety.

Why are we so afraid to be real just when people need us the most?
The thought gripped me as I lay there, full of an ugly, life-
threatening cancer, similar to that which held Barbara.

And cancer is not the only devastating illness.

Now I was on the other side of the gap, walking in the
"alien land" of illness that few friends or loved ones know
how to enter. Already I had experienced many sincere but
misdirected attempts to help. And I'd also discovered a few
rare friends and relatives who really knew how to show their
concern in this trying time.

*People need to know specifically how to reach out to a friend who is
seriously ill.* The thought would not leave me.

Could I help people to understand? Was I strong enough
to share my very personal interactions—good and bad, sad or
funny?

From that moment, I knew I had to try.

2

Facing Up

Only a morbid person would dwell on the thought that we all have a limited span of time on earth. Our heads are whirling with lively plans for our families and careers, with vital interests in music, sports, art, travel. We embrace life— and rightly so.

And then a friend or spouse or child is stricken with a life-threatening illness. At once, with little warning, we are facing up to death.

Before you can begin to help, it's crucial to understand how your friend may feel after a doctor's serious pronouncement. So much is going on under the surface. A few remarkable folks I've known have faced the possibility of sickness or death with great calm. Many more are caught in a great internal wrestling match.

That's how it was for me. One moment I was healthy, the mother of two fine girls, happily active in the Presbyterian Church in Newton, Massachusetts, where my husband Monty was the new senior pastor. And the next moment my entire life was being yanked out of my hands. All it took was one diagnosis.

The thoughts and feelings are so immense, personal and deep. Most folks find it terrifically hard to open up. Let me pull back the curtain a bit and allow you a glimpse.

We had just moved East from California, and fall was settling in red and gold on the New England hardwoods. Monty had previously worked with Young Life, a ministry to teenagers, and then held an associate pastorate. Now he was responsible for leading a church, and I was eager to help. It was our ministry.

As I hung wallpaper in our new home, a heavy, lingering fatigue sank into my bones. My muscles ached as if I'd over-stretched. Just three months earlier, my doctor had given me a clean bill of health, so I passed it off as the strain of moving.

Winter blew in. Suzanne and Marybeth, then twelve and ten, both loved the snow. We lugged our sleds up a steep hill nearby. But as I made my first "run," bumping down the slope on my stomach, I felt an unusual discomfort.

By March, the tenderness and swelling could not be ignored. A series of X-rays followed, and my doctor sent them to be read by a specialist, Dr. Peter Mozden. An appointment was scheduled.

When Monty and I read the plate on Dr. Mozden's door, we were shocked. It read: "Surgeon, Gynecologist, Oncologist." A cancer specialist!

In the waiting room, I glanced at the other patients, wondering which ones had "it."

Dr. Mozden showed us the telltale X-rays, pointing out the mass that appeared to fill my abdominal cavity. His face was grave.

"We must schedule surgery immediately. In fact, I'll arrange it for next Monday," he said firmly, and I knew I had little choice in the matter. "Possibly it's an ovarian cyst. But the size indicates a probable malignancy."

Malignancy! I tried to hurl that word away from me like a live grenade.

For the next few days, even as the pain grew, I struggled

to believe the best. But Thursday night, the pain billowed unbearably. Monty dialed an emergency number. It was exactly the kind of scene I'd dreaded.

An ambulance pulled up with red lights flashing. Monty woke the girls, who sat sleepy-eyed and confused as a neighbor rushed in to stay with them. The last thing I saw as they slid my stretcher into the ambulance was Suzanne, wrapped in her favorite old quilt and watching me from Marybeth's upstairs window.

All the rest was a blur of pain. I felt my life go spinning out of my control.

I half-woke from surgery. A gastrointestinal tube ran through one nasal passage and irritated the back of my throat. My mouth was parched. I stirred a little, and at once Monty's face was close to mine.

"Monty," I struggled to speak around the tube, "do I have cancer?"

Not trusting his own ability to speak, he nodded sadly. Then his shoulders shook with convulsing sobs.

I closed my eyes and a huge weight settled into my chest.

I lay alone in the dark, staring up at the barren ceiling. A night nurse passed by the door, and all was still. Monty had long since gone home to the girls.

Dr. Mozden's afternoon visit was fresh in my mind.

"The cancer has advanced far into stage three. The mass is stuck to all your vital organs, which would be in jeopardy should we attempt surgical removal."

He advised immediate, aggressive chemotherapy—and then explained the odds. It was worth fighting, he said, but my condition was normally considered "incurable."

I may die. The thought stung.

I never had thought much about dying—not in relation to myself. Only a few times had death's lightning struck close enough to startle me with its thunder.

When I was in high school, a classmate was playing basketball when she lost her balance and fell into the window of a partition door. The glass shattered, and a long, narrow piece slashed at her jugular vein. She died almost instantly.

Later in life, death struck much closer. The hurt and loss were far deeper. At 77, Dad was still the witty, sometimes dogmatic, kind and godly father I'd always loved. Though he still kept up his retirement home in Pennsylvania, he was slowing down noticeably. One day the phone call came: Dad was gone.

My brothers and sisters, who lived near Dad, met me at the airport when I arrived from the West Coast. Just before the funeral, we found an unfinished note to one of Dad's sisters. He had penned these words: "I think I am about to go home."

And home he went. The thought comforted me the last time I looked on his face: *Dad is at home in heaven.*

For a while I struggled with tremendous feelings of grief and loss. Eventually, my faith brought peace. I rested in the knowledge that, for the Christian, death is the continuation of an incredible journey. Dad was in a lovely, permanent dwelling place.

Now I was still staring at the ceiling in my hospital room. The nurse passed my door again, her crepe-soled shoes squeaking on the polished floor.

This time I was the one who might be leaving for another "home." But I didn't *want* to go. I wasn't ready yet.

Snatches of poems came to mind—from Tennyson's "Crossing the Bar," and Wordsworth's "Ode to Immortality." Certain books had also influenced my image of death. Mentally I searched the pages of Frances Hodgson Burnett's *The Secret Garden, Hind's Feet on High Places* by Hannah Hurnard, *Behold Your God* by Agnes Sanford, Thornton Wilder's *Our Town*. In *The Last Battle*, C.S. Lewis referred to death as "higher up and further in." And of course the Bible describes the golden streets of an eternal city where no tears are shed.

The gravity of the earth was incredibly strong—even if the golden streets of heaven were awaiting my footfalls. Sure, I wanted to embark on that adventure—someday. But I wasn't ready for a one-way ticket for one.

A warm spill of tears slid out of the corners of my eyes, into my hair. For me, leaving my family was the true issue.

Monty was at the peak of his life's calling. Eighteen years of marriage had blended us together—two distinctly different personalities. Our love had matured in creative conflict. We were inseparable. How could I leave him in the prime of life?

Tucked into my thought was a desolating kind of guilt. I would be leaving Monty with two young daughters to raise. The very thought of Suzanne and Marybeth ached inside me.

Suzanne was riding an adolescent roller coaster of emotions. Marybeth was already independent, such a lover of life and a natural survivor. Strangely, I had more instinctive peace about leaving her than either Monty or Suzanne.

If only I could see them through the next few years—to make it smoother for them. Even as I began bargaining with God, I knew I was bargaining for my own sake, too. My family was young, needing a woman's love. And I wanted to enjoy them.

I found that my hand was clutching the metal side rail of the hospital bed. Relaxing, I took a deep breath to calm myself.

What if I lie here in pain, suffering and useless to my family? What if I become a burden to them and not a pleasure? Do I really want them to interrupt their lives, trekking night after night to watch me disintegrate?

At length, a new resolve took over. *No,* I decided, *I must die quickly and easily.*

My internal wrestling match had worn me to the verge of sleep. A depression, black and heavy as coal, settled on me as I closed my eyes at last.

Fortunately, God had already prepared some friends who knew exactly how to come and lighten my crushing load.

3

Learning to Listen

Helping your friend to open up and talk about his or her illness is one of the greatest gifts you can give. Like lancing a boil, though, it takes directness *and* sensitivity. I learned this the hard way.

Several years before our family moved from California to West Newton, Massachusetts, a young friend named Pam who attended our church was struck with Hodgkin's disease, cancer of the lymph system. Of course the word "cancer" evoked in me a horror. Cancer meant that she might die.

One evening, she and her five-year-old son came to our house to dinner. Seeing Pam's little boy laughing and eating with my own children awakened something in me. Again and again, I thought of the fact that he might soon be motherless. Suddenly, I felt all the pain and fear Pam must have been suffering.

After we'd finished at the table, the children disappeared to a far corner of the house, while Monty slipped away to make some necessary phone calls. Filling two mugs with steaming coffee, we settled comfortably in the living room.

Immediately, I set the conversation off on an ordinary, nonthreatening course. We both taught English, and I heard myself asking several innocuous questions about Pam's experience in our mutual profession. Eventually, the conversation turned to the joys of raising children, and, finally, to some of the new classes being offered at our church.

But inside me, a pressure was mounting. Watching her, listening to her talk, the questions were pounding. I wanted, deeply wanted to ask, "Pam, what's it really like—the chemotherapy, the life-and-death battle that's being fought right in your own body?" But the words were aborted in my brain.

Soon the children popped back into the room, interrupting our quiet. Then Monty rejoined us. I had missed a God-given opportunity to help Pam work through some tough, personal struggles—to help validate her personhood.

The opportunity never came again. And I have had to walk through my own suffering to see my mistake. Now as a cancer victim myself, I am often faced with the difficult task of avoiding any talk about my illness in order to put others at ease when I ache for them to be real with me.

Some days I am eager to talk about my feelings, my treatments, the boredom of lying flat on my back in the hospital, my concern for Monty and the girls. Some days I am just tired of thinking about cancer at all. I never know which mood I'll be in. But I would be delighted to have my friend ask me bluntly what I *feel* like talking about.

From all these experiences, I've learned that some preliminary work is necessary before you go to visit a sick friend.

In most cases, we have to learn how to say, out loud, the name of the illness. It's harder than you think. In Pam's case, I ought to have practiced saying the words "cancer" or "Hodgkin's disease." Forming these words beforehand would have kept them from sticking in my throat.

On the other hand, it's best to avoid words like "terminal," which leave no room for God's possible intervention.

Fortunately for me, I have also been blessed with some

wonderful friends whose gentleness and true concern would open up anyone's heart.

Judy, for example, taught me that you don't have to be a close friend necessarily before you reach out to someone who's ill. She was living in Boston only temporarily while her husband finished his post-grad work in dentistry there. She had quickly involved herself in our church, and refused to be intimidated by the fact that we hardly knew each other.

Dropping in to visit one morning, she admitted, "I don't know you very well. But I know that you *must* need a friend right now. I don't have anything much to say, but at least I can listen."

Those were just the right words, and she proved true to them. All through our talk, she gave me her undivided attention. I knew that she was with me, that she really did want to know how things were going.

Another good listener and valuable friend is Dennis Doerr, the associate pastor of our church. In his many visits, especially, he provided me with two keys to the art of listening.

Dennis came to my hospital room within days of my first operation, before my treatments began. His brows were knitted together slightly, overshadowing his gentle smile with a look of genuine concern. He perched on the edge of the chair by my bed and I knew, of course, that Monty had already told him about the doctor's findings.

He squeezed my hand in a short, polite greeting. Then gently, directly, he got to the heart of things.

"Betsy, how are you accepting the surgical results?" he asked, leaning close to me.

My answer was a long time in coming. Dennis waited patiently, not hurrying on to another topic out of embarrassment. When my response did come, it took a long time to get out all that I needed to express—partly because I was tired, partly because I was sorting through so many thoughts.

Dennis continued to listen intently for as long as it took me to answer the question—which was quite some time. He knew that I needed to get the whole thing—the mixed feelings of hope and depression—completely washed out of my system. As I reeled out my inner self, his compassionate eyes never left mine.

Only when I had thoroughly explained my emotional sledride did he move on to another important topic.

"What lies ahead with the treatments?"

I was off again. Occasionally, he would stop me and ask a question as I explained, so unclearly at first, the process of chemotherapy. Even his questions showed me he was truly interested—that he was with me.

It was the first of many visits that Dennis paid me. Each time, he came with real interest in what I had to say.

This is the first key to good listening. Don't go with a set "agenda."

Once, an older friend came to visit. She asked how I was feeling, and before I'd gotten out half-a-sentence, she launched into a twenty-minute story about her recent visit with her grandchildren. That was what she had "prepared" to talk about in order to fill up the visit.

So it's important that you let your sick friend set the agenda. It only takes a few times for someone to ask about me, then move on before I'd answered, and I get the message: they don't really want to hear about me. Soon I withdraw.

The second key to listening that I learned from Dennis Doerr is how to listen actively. This takes direct eye contact, real concentration. It means following your friend's train of thought—even if it's a jumpy one.

For instance, serious illness is very confining. Your

friend maybe bedridden in a hospital or housebound for quite
some time. When you ask, "How are you feeling?" the
response may well be, "Bored."

At this point, don't shift the conversation to a self-
centered—and, frankly, unwelcome—rundown of all the
latest movies you've seen and outdoor sports you've enjoyed.

Pursue your friend's boredom. Find out if he or she
would like some magazines to read or needlework to do. Arrange visits with a group of friends on a schedule, keeping in
mind your friend's limited physical stamina, hospital regula-
tions and personal needs of the family. In many cases, boredom is brought on by the idea that life has gone on without
you, that no one else cares to be with you where you are.

Emotions are an important area that your friend may
wish to talk about. Keep in mind that this is tender ground.

Sometimes people ask, "How does going through all this
make you *feel?*" My response might be general: "Miserable."

At such a time, special friends will help to pinpoint the
emotion as a first step in dealing with it. In the course of
conversation, you might ask: "Does your illness make you
angry?" "Are you lonely?" Questions that could open the
door further might be: "What are you worried about the
most?" "What are your greatest needs?"

Of course, feelings are not just emotional. Your friend is
quite likely experiencing genuine physical discomfort. Pain.
Hearing about the physical details of illness might be tough,
but I truly value my "unflinching" friends.

My friend Dierdre asked me one day, "What do you *do*
with all those hours of being sick?" Perhaps she thought I'd
talk about reading books, but I needed to answer on another
level.

Very matter-of-factly, I looked at her. "Mostly, I crawl
into bed exhausted. Sometimes I drop off to sleep. More often

I just lie there with thoughts running through my mind and"—my shoulders sagged with the unpleasantness of the truth—"then the next attack of vomiting hits me."

Dierdre shook her head, but she didn't flinch. I felt that she was actually trying to get inside my skin, to understand the intensity of my treatments. In some way, she was identifying with my weakness. Gently, she said, "It must be awful to feel like you're turning inside-out."

After she left, I recognized that Dierdre might have chosen to shift the conversation to something a bit more pleasant. It wouldn't have been difficult. But she kept all self-centered comments out of the conversation, knowing there would be other times for light talk and pleasantries.

And it's not unlikely that your sick friend may come up with a good day. Emotions come under control, spirits become healthy and vital again, some illnesses even go into remission as mine did for a time. Everyone is glad to hear a sick one say that he is truly doing "fine."

Again, this is not a signal to launch off on a long personal history. Don't fill up the time with your plans and chatter. Get your friend to talk about his or her plans. Maybe it's a longing to visit the beauty parlor. Or it could be a desire to talk about how good it feels to be back in a normal family routine. It might be a planned trip to the lake, an evening on the town or a chance to go to a ballgame. In any case, remember that the agenda belongs to your friend.

Not all, but most people who are faced with a debilitating illness become acutely aware of the spiritual dimension of their lives. Your friend may never have thought much about God, an afterlife or his own spirit before the onset of illness. Or perhaps your friend has already developed a strong, lively faith. In either case, sickness is truly a spiritual battle—a time of struggle, questioning and discovering, maybe for the first time, the true strength of your faith.

To me, this is such a crucial area that I have devoted two chapters to it further on.

In listening to your friend, you may discover still another possibility. Your friend may not want to talk about illness or deeply personal matters at all. Some people find it difficult to open up. Others share themselves only selectively. If this is the case, don't force the issue.

A woman I knew in California, named Rubie, exuded a warm, positive, bright spirit all during her bout with an illness that eventually took her life. All of us who knew her and loved her delighted in that joyful personality, which was strong to the end.

But some of us grew concerned that she never ever talked about her impending death. She could share her day-by-day struggles, and talk about her pain. She could even name her ailment. But we were never able to draw out her thoughts about death, which we all knew was imminent, barring a miracle.

I discussed this with Monty one evening, and he was not at all concerned. As a clergyman, he was a member of a Cancer Recovery Group that Rubie attended.

"Oh, she talks about death a great deal," he assured me. "She has a deep peace about it. Rubie shares her feelings, but she's like a lot of people—she shares selectively."

In the context of that group, my friend felt comfortable to express herself openly. Apparently Rubie never felt the need to bring that element into her closer friendships. In her case, had some of us forced the issue, it may have caused pain and not healing.

On the other end of the scale, one friend decided to question me until she forced me into an intimacy. I'm certain she meant well when she appointed herself to be my confidant. And in the beginning, when my thought-life was consumed with accepting the reality of my illness, I appreciated her concern. But when I was released from the hospital, and grew strong enough to get involved again in normal activities and routines, I did not want to go over the old ground.

Yet whenever this friend spotted me across a room, she'd make her way to my side and inwardly I'd cringe because I knew what she was going to ask. In the midst of the happiest, lightest conversation about cooking or children or the church, she would pose the same gloomy questions: "How are you feeling? Is your illness progressing?"

I became annoyed. At that time, I needed people to treat me, as much as possible, like a person who had a normal, productive, creative life apart from the fact that I happened to be battling cancer. Unfortunately, I was no longer Betsy Burnham to this woman, I was "the lady who has cancer." My sickness was the only thing on her agenda, even when it wasn't on mine.

To sum it up, listening is one of the first, best steps in helping your friend to win the emotional, mental and spiritual battles that accompany illness. A listening friend faces your inner struggles with you, bearing the burden at your side, leaving you with more energy to fight the battle for life.

4

From the Heart

In the Old Testament book of Ecclesiastes, the most beautiful, uplifting and most oft-quoted passage is the one that begins: "To everything there is a season, and a time to every purpose under the heaven" (Ecclesiastes 3:1, KJV).

In that same passage, the author wisely tells us about "a time to keep silence, and a time to speak" (verse 7).

Certainly, your time spent with a friend who is seriously ill will involve more than listening. Listening is the first step, and tells you what you need to address. It wins you the right and the "time to speak."

The most meaningful and touching words that any friend said to me were not the glib maxims: "Cheer up. Things will get better." That just doesn't do it. Some of my friends are gifted, not only with "active listening," but they are able to speak from the heart, too.

Dorothy Jayne, a wise and longtime friend, taught me so much about blending these two necessary aspects of friendship.

When she received the news about my diagnosis, Dorothy boarded the first cross-country flight for Boston. A psychiatric social worker and family counselor, Dorothy has been an emotional pillar of strength that Monty and I have valued throughout our entire ministry.

She sat by my hospital bed for a few long evenings, and we talked. I was weak and could only share in brief snatches

my feelings about my own future, my concern for Monty—
and especially for Suzanne and Marybeth. I was too worn out
physically and emotionally to grasp most of what she said in
response at first.

But one relaxed afternoon, Dorothy sat by my bed
reflecting on her life. It had been tough, but the hard times
built in her a strong Christian character and sensitivity that
were always evident. Somehow she knew just what was on
my mind at that moment.

"Betsy, I was thirteen years old when my mother died of
cancer," Dorothy reminded me. She reached over and slipped
her warm hand into mine.

I had known about Dorothy's mother once. How was it
I'd forgotten?

This wise and wonderful woman had been nurtured
through her teen years by the love of God Himself. If the Lord
could mold such a beautiful personality once by His love and
presence and power—and without the aid of a mother—I
knew He could lead my girls in His perfect way, too.

I was staring at our linked hands, and suddenly Dorothy's strength and character seemed to fill me as if an electric
current were passing through her fingers into mine. I knew
that it wasn't easy for her to visit me and dredge up the
memories of her own mother's illness and death.

My eyes brimmed over. Dorothy's ministry to me on this
trip was accomplished. My spirit rested, genuinely trusting
God in that moment.

But it wasn't only my close friends who touched me. In
our mobile society, you may not have had years to build such a
close relationship as I have with Dorothy. Even a new
acquaintance can reach out to someone by saying the right
word at the right moment.

Shortly after Dorothy's visit, a nurse who was new on

the floor came in to introduce herself. She was young, and smiled with an unusual radiance that was invigorating. Even though she could have read my chart and learned all that was "professionally" necessary to know about me, she deliberately took the time to ask about my family and my particular type of cancer.

Briefly, I told her about the doctor's diagnosis and the projected treatments. Perhaps she noticed the catch in my voice when I mentioned my family and the ages of our daughters.

When I finished, her gentle eyes were still locked with mine. Then she spoke in a soft, unthreatening voice.

"When I was fifteen, Mom died. It was hard," she confessed, "but we made it. The whole family had to pull together. We all shared the work load. And yet I think I maintained a normal teenage life.

"I'm married now, and have a child. I can see that those things I learned when Mom was sick—and after she'd gone—have made me a better mother, wife and nurse."

She didn't have to say any more. I knew that what she said was true because she was demonstrating her strength and love. Again, I breathed a grateful, silent prayer to my heavenly Father for sending the person with the right words.

Both of these friends spoke to me from the heart, and that made all the difference. Carefully, they had picked up what was most on my mind at that moment—Suzanne and Marybeth and their future.

They showed empathy, not sentimental sympathy. They had experienced a side of life very much like what I was going through, but they didn't preach or give me a "pep talk." Directly and delicately, they reminded me that even in illness and loss, bad can be turned into good under God's watch and care.

But suppose you and your family have never experienced the drawn-out battle of a life-threatening illness? That doesn't mean you have no common ground on which to relate to your sick friend. But it is best to find the level on which you *can* relate.

Remember that many feelings get wrapped into an illness: loneliness, fear, sadness, uselessness, guilt, anger, frustration. All of us have had these feelings at times, and with varying intensity. These are the areas of common ground to listen for.

Maybe your friend will let you know that he is fearful about an upcoming surgery or treatment. And perhaps you have felt an overpowering fear for a child, spouse, parent, or even for your own life. You might look for an opportunity to tell about that experience briefly. Be prepared to answer questions honestly, and remember not to keep the rest of the conversation focused on yourself.

I realize that this level of communication is not easy for some people. I have often encountered real stiffness in this area of heart-to-heart sharing. Some folks are not used to showing their emotions. Others are afraid to be vulnerable or to appear weak, less than perfect or not in control.

One evening, a young couple who are good friends of mine came to visit me. After a moment or two of pleasantries, they asked me how everything was going.

It so happened that I'd just received some discouraging news. The treatments were not slowing the spread of cancer as hoped. I didn't have the strength to cover up my disappointment.

As I repeated the doctor's report, the woman's eyes welled up with tears, which spilled down her cheeks. Immediately she began to apologize, "I didn't want to cry like this. I'm sorry. I feel so awful."

Her husband sat nervously on the windowsill, shifting positions every few seconds. Finally he confessed, "I feel so uncomfortable. I have no idea what to say."

They didn't have to *say* anything. They had come. Their love and concern shouted to me. I assured my young friend that she could have done far worse than to cry in my presence.

The truly unfortunate folks were those who stayed away altogether, as in the case of another young friend who approached me recently.

"All the time you were in the hospital, I wanted to come and see you," he began. Then his face reddened. "But I didn't come—because I was afraid I would cry."

The truth is, all of us are a combination of strengths and weaknesses. I am not suggesting that you have to have an all-out, towel-wringing cry to show your friend that you truly care. But you can enter that deeper level of friendship that some folks miss when they deny or suppress emotions.

The most satisfying relationships develop when you have shifted from hearing *facts* to hearing *feelings*. The deepest communication takes place after the specifics of prognosis, treatments and symptoms are all spelled out. Then involuntary feelings can emerge as part of the true conversation.

Granted, it's much easier for us to hear and respond to positive, happy circumstances. I have a number of wonderful friends I can talk to when I'm hopeful, energetic, patient or cheerful. And I'm always glad for their happy encouragement. But it's the special friends who know how to respond to my anger, resentment, discouragement, fear and grief.

Many people, even our closest friends, may find it hard to respond to negative emotions. The problem is that somehow many of us have been conditioned to give superficial responses at the most sensitive moments. Just when our friend is having a bad time and needs to hear from our heart, we give a canned response.

One of the most vivid and unhappy examples was the day I visited a Christian woman who was dying. She was weak and in great pain. In the middle of our talk, a woman named Sue came in and stood at the foot of her bed.

"Listen, don't worry," Sue offered. "Everything is going to be all right. It's such a beautiful day outside. If you'll just learn to keep your chin up and think about nice things, you'll be out of here and home before you know it."

I was stunned by Sue's response to the situation, and I felt sorry for her at the same time. It was obvious that our friend was *not* going to leave the hospital. (In fact, within three weeks she died.) Since her faith was solid, everything was going to be "all right" in the eternal sense. But in the here and now, she was suffering.

In fairness to Sue, I suppose she simply could not empathize with any of our friend's emotions at that moment. Maybe she had never learned to open herself to such deep feelings. But her strong optimism did more harm than good. If she could not enter into our friend's grief, she might have just held her hand or gently rubbed her sore back. These simple acts of love would have communicated her concern much better than empty words.

Always keep in mind that positive or negative emotions are better expressed than hidden. Allow yourself to feel, and don't be afraid to express yourself.

Just knowing that friends truly care about me, and feel my up-and-down emotions along with me, has often rekindled my old fight and determination when living with illness gets tough.

All this is not to deny that *strength* can be expressed emotionally, too. It may be particularly difficult for the family of your sick friend to cope with the teetering emotions because they are so close to the situation. If others are shaky emotionally, your friend may need you for support and encouragement.

I know of one unhappy instance where a young friend had to rely solely on the emotional support of strangers when doctors first told him they suspected leukemia.

He was living away from home, working at one of his first jobs out of college. Increasing fatigue was his first warning signal, which he ignored. This was followed by prolonged and painful glandular swellings in his throat. He visited the doctor, expecting to hear that he had some sort of minor infection.

When the doctors offered their diagnosis, this young man told no one in his own family for months, though he readily asked for prayer and support from new-found Christian friends—people he hardly knew. He explained it this way.

"My mom has been a 'worrier' her whole life. As a result, she suffers from internal bleeding. Whenever things get rocky, Mom's condition is aggravated—and suddenly, we have to worry about her health on top of whatever challenge we're facing.

"I decided that I'd rather live on my own as long as possible, without telling my family, rather than bearing the emotional strain of her upset, too."

Fortunately, Christian friends convinced him it was important to let his own family in on the news, no matter how upsetting. Their strength helped him to deal with his own illness—and with a touchy, long-standing problem in relation to his own parents. They shared his emotions, they understood his feelings about his family *and* they encouraged him while he faced a doubly tough situation.

How beautiful and welcome it is to hear the encouraging,

strengthening words of a friend—one who speaks from the heart.

And yet there is a deeper, more crucial level where your friend may need to receive your care. I am talking about the spirit. The spirit of a person is often compared to a well of water. The spirit can be a source of flowing joy and inner strength or, as in the case of serious illness, it can threaten to dry up.

5

The Five Faces of the Seriously Ill

I don't know where the teaching comes from that a Christian should never express negative emotions. I certainly don't find it in the Bible.

Job, who complained bitterly about his pain and loss, still maintained an iron grip on his knowledge of God's omnipotence. His best friends were shocked and embarrassed by his complaints and tried to silence him, but Job still cried, "Though he slay me, yet will I trust in him" (Job 13:15, KJV). And in the end, it was Job who was given the deeper, more awesome understanding of God.

David, the king of Israel, expressed the heights and depths of emotion in his psalms, the greatest praise and devotional literature of all time. His anguish seems as deep, fervent and intense as his joy is high and unbridled. And yet he never seems guilty for not being "more positive."

I've come to believe strongly that God understands our feelings. He doesn't turn His back when we are weak or hurt or depressed; He walks with us right where we are. He allows us the *dignity* to have our own feelings. And all the time, He is gently, patiently waiting to point us toward wholeness when we are ready to receive it.

Right after my initial surgery, Monty found himself weighted with a sudden, unexpected load. On top of the emotional stress, he had to cope with a normal work schedule, plus a household that needed to run in a semblance of order and make daily visits to see me in the hospital. Physically he was exhausted, and soon he was submerged in depression. I would describe his condition as "partial paralysis."

Many dear people surrounded us right away, supporting us with prayer and helping in loving, practical ways. But others found it difficult to see their pastor—their spiritual leader—struggling with the negative feelings that accompany depression.

Always honest, Monty would admit when he was discouraged or anxious or upset or hurting. He needed the strength of the "bones and muscles" of the Christian body at that moment.

Fairly often he heard this kind of salt-rubbing response: "I'm worried about you. You need to change your attitude and put your trust in God." And sometimes it didn't have to be spoken; it was communicated with a look.

Monty hadn't lost his faith. His deep trust in God was not in danger. But he needed to be free to express his emotions, negative or positive, to those close to him without a sense of guilt.

If you are to be sensitive to the seriously ill, please let this person express all the feelings that churn on the inside. It might help to know that you may find this sufferer in one of five stages. Be aware of them if you truly want to be helpful.

The first phase your friend may enter is *denial*—denial that his life is in jeopardy. Denial is perfectly normal, a temporary protection from the pain of reality when the mind is fending off the conscious thought of death.

For four or five days after my surgery and diagnosis, I would wake with the same thoughts running through my head: "It's all a bad dream. They've made a mistake. I'll wake up later and find it isn't true." Then I'd go back to sleep.

In this first phase, I was recovering from the physical

trauma of surgery. It was a temporary resting place before the coming spiritual battles. At this point I leaned on certain Scripture passages.

So I suggest bringing a Bible to the seriously ill person you visit, marked with passages that highlight God's steadfast, eternal nature. Here are a few:

"Jesus Christ is the same yesterday and today and forever" (Hebrews 13:8).

In the Psalms, David assures us that God's love is ever fresh and new, always available like a spring of clear, cold water: "Your love, O Lord, reaches to the heavens, your faithfulness to the skies . . . How priceless is your unfailing love!" (Psalm 36:5, 7).

The wonderfully exuberant Psalm 100 ends with this fascinating promise: "For the Lord is good and his love endures forever; his faithfulness continues through all generations" (Psalm 100:5).

"The Lord delights," David tells us, "in those . . . who put their hope in his unfailing love" (Psalm 147:11).

"The grass withers and the flowers fall, but the word of our God stands forever" (Isaiah 40:8).

For me, the only way to deal with my illness was to stop denying it and face my own mortality—to deal with life and death. But I, like most people, tried to *bargain* away my disease.

Bargaining is often the second phase of illness.

I prayed like this: "God, if only You will heal me, I will accept all of the speaking engagements, teach all the Bible studies or Sunday school classes ever requested of me, and attend every church function for the rest of my life."

In short, I was haggling with Him as if He were a vendor in a market place—which He is not. Just as I could do nothing to earn my salvation (see Ephesians 2:8-9), so there was nothing I could do to merit healing. His gifts flow out of His graceful nature. Frantically bargaining with God is to take matters into one's own hands, to forget His very nature.

Certainly we should ask God for healing. But along with this prayer of faith, we need to accept God's final authority in the matter.

The apostle Paul went through this. He suffered "a thorn in my flesh" (II Corinthians 12:7), then went on to ask three times for God to remove his affliction. Finally, this response came from the Lord: "My grace is sufficient for you, for my power is made perfect in weakness" (verse 9). And so Paul learned in his weakness to rely on God's strength as a gift!

Now, whenever I visit sick friends who are in the bargaining stage, I remind them that God is in control. And I point out passages such as James 1:17, "Every good and perfect gift is from above, coming down from the Father of the heavenly lights, who does not change like shifting shadows." Then I pray that my suffering friend will rest, knowing that God freely gives His gifts of healing or strength for the battle.

The third stage, *anger,* is perhaps the most difficult emotion to face for the seriously ill person. Like other emotions, it comes without our willing it. Yet we can control our anger and decide what to do with it; in fact, Scripture tells us, "Do not let the sun go down while you are still angry" (Ephesians 4:26).

If you sense anger is simmering under the surface, help your friend to express it. All it takes is a gentle recognition that it is there, which gives the sick person the freedom to let it out. Those friends who allowed me to vent my anger not only provided me a valuable pressure valve, but also helped me to avoid a long-term anger, which can become a virile inner sickness that eats away inner strength.

Ultimately, all anger is directed at God, since He has final control in everything. If your friend is wrestling, openly or unconsciously, with anger against God, try to help him to understand that God is not our opponent. God is on our side. When all earthly help has vanished, He is always there.

David says this beautifully: "I lift up my eyes to the hills—where does my help come from? My help comes from the Lord, the Maker of heaven and earth" (Psalm 121:1-2). There is no need to wrestle against the very one who is "our refuge and strength, an ever present help in trouble" (Psalm 46:1).

Depression is the fourth phase of this internal progression. It is always difficult to deal with. Your sick friend may simply become silent and listless, as I did. I kept my thoughts to myself. In the hospital, I sat quietly in the corner of my room, not caring to know other patients. I was too low to tell my feelings to anyone, though every night when the lights were out, I soaked my pillow with tears. Even after I was released to go home, the depression didn't lift. I sat outside in a deck chair and stared into space.

Depression can involve so many factors. After all, how would you feel if you found out today that you might not live to see your children graduate from high school? Or that your life's goals would never be reached? What if you saw your own pain and suffering mirrored in the eyes of the one you loved best? Or that months and years were rushing by as you sat hour after hour in a doctor's office, a hospital bed or alone at home?

If your friend's depression stretches into weeks or months without any sign of letting up, try to get his or her family to seek professional help. Be sure that your friend's doctor and minister are aware of the situation.

This is not to say that your help and constant encouragement are without value. You are the one who may be readily available when a pastor or doctor is tied up with other appointments. If your friend is willing to see you, you might read brief passages from Scripture. Again, the Psalms can touch your friend's emotional depths.

"The Lord is my shepherd," David proclaims in Psalm 23. What a gentle, reassuring image of our Lord! And there is more.

"He restores my soul . . . Even though I walk through the valley of the shadow of death, I will fear no evil, for you are with me" (Psalm 23:3-4). In these emotionally desolate moments, your friend needs a gentle reminder that God is still there—even though the joy and every sense of His presence may have gone cold.

Psalm 139 says that God knows everything about us—where we are, what we feel and think—since He created our "inmost being" (verse 13). There is no place where God is not. If we are in heaven or in the depths, whether enjoying moments of sunlight or surrounded by darkness, He is there. He walks with us in everything.

Paul echoes this psalm in Romans. The apostle, who suffered much himself, asks, "Who shall separate us from the love of Christ? Shall trouble or hardship or persecution or famine or nakedness or danger or sword?" (Romans 8:35). His resounding answer is this: "I am convinced that neither death nor life, neither angels nor demons, neither the present nor the future, nor any powers, neither height nor depth, nor anything else in all creation, will be able to separate us from the love of God that is in Christ Jesus our Lord" (verses 38-39).

Not even a dry, hard-packed wall of depression can stop God from loving your friend. For the sick person, it is important to remember that God and others still love with great intensity, even when the sick one can feel nothing but numbness.

Not all of the phases of illness are negative. Sooner or later, your friend may enter stage five and *accept* his illness. That doesn't mean that he will be happy about it. Acceptance is relaxing; some would describe it as finding peace.

Acceptance certainly does not mean throwing up one's hands in defeat, admitting that death is imminent. It is not lying back and giving up. That is only self-fulfilling prophecy. Accepting illness means that you are ready to deal with the situation at hand—to stop worrying about tomorrow and its troubles and enter into the physical, spiritual battle of today.

At this point, it is a good idea to encourage the sufferer to "put on the full armor of God" (Ephesians 6:10-18), and begin to cooperate with God in the real faith battle so that "when the day of evil comes, you may be able to stand your ground, and after you have done everything, to stand" (Ephesians 6:13).

The peace that comes through acceptance will always be tested by enemy forces. So the ill one must be prepared for a life-and-death battle. The phases of his warfare repeat again and again. Be ready to step in as a reinforcement, even if it seems that you've watched the same struggle before. One day, your friend may exhibit a relaxed faith, only to be pitched headlong into depression again the following day.

The unexpected, small things can catch you unawares, just when you thought you were finished with the fight.

I remember looking at a gymnastics meet on television one evening. As I watched the young athletes compete on the parallel bars, the flying rings and the "horse," I became totally engrossed in these events on the screen before me.

Suddenly, a fury gripped me, and I threw the T.V.'s remote control unit against the footboard of the hospital bed. Irrationally, I was furious at these healthy, strong young athletes that could flaunt their rippling muscles, their agility and coordination, while a tumor was swelling in my abdomen and I was so weak I could hardly walk. After a prayer for help, I retrieved the control unit and a little of my composure.

One of the final armaments that Paul gives in his list of spiritual "weaponry" is prayer. He tells us, "Be alert and always keep on praying" (Ephesians 6:18).

Yet praying for the sick, as I will try to show in the next chapter, is still uncertain territory for many Christians.

6

The Prayer of Faith

"Your visitors are here," the nurse announced from the doorway with a hint of impatience in her voice. She stepped back into the hallway, eyeing my five friends with disapproval as they filed into my room.

"Hi, Betsy." They circled my bed, greeting me one by one with a touch, smiles, a peck on the cheek. A look of excitement passed between us now that all the "conspirators" were together.

It had taken special permission to have all five friends admitted to my room at the same time. Neighbors and friends from church had fairly flocked in to see me. And I was still recuperating from major surgery, trying to pick up some strength before my battery of treatments. It was no wonder the nurses were uneasy about this added flood of visitors.

Besides, this was no ordinary social call. These friends had come to my hospital room to pray for my healing from malignant cancer.

A few months before, I would have looked askance at our group. More than one close friend had become seriously ill and begun to pray for a complete healing. But I could only pray for relief of their pain, for strength to endure, and that they would have peace to handle their plight. I was reluctant to go beyond those qualities, thinking that they were too sick to get well; even prayer could not help so grave a situation.

47

Suddenly I was the one confined to a hospital bed. My position was uncomfortably similar to those friends for whom I had given up hope. Now I, too, was asking God: *How should I respond? Are You going to make me well?*

I knew that the New Testament instructs Christians to act in faith on behalf of the one who is ill. "Is any one of you sick? He should call the elders of the church to pray over him and anoint him with oil in the name of the Lord" (James 5:14).

Even before my surgery, the elders of our church asked if they could anoint me, lay on hands and pray. I agreed; surely they could do no harm. I recalled many, many incidents in Scripture when Jesus healed miraculously.

But physical healing now? In the twentieth century? I wasn't hopeful.

Then came the surgery, and the prognosis: malignancy. Suddenly, I had an intense personal desire for healing.

Now this group of five friends were gathered at my bedside to pray. In the past, each one had told me about a physical healing they had experienced personally or witnessed in a friend. At the time I'd listened without really hearing.

Watching them now, I was intent on their every word. Their eyes and voices were alive with faith. Tipping a small bottle of oil onto his fingers, one man reached down and gently anointed my forehead. A tiny trickle slid into my eyebrow, and they began to pray in turn.

"Lord," one began, softly but fervently, "penetrate each cell and tissue of Betsy's body with your light and power. Dissolve this inoperable tumor."

Another man prayed in a different direction, asking for my "deliverance." "I discern an evil spirit of destruction, deluge and death at work here. Drive it away, Lord."

They *really* had my attention now.

Another prayed, "Satan's attack on Betsy must be thwarted, Lord."

The next morning I awoke, filled with a sense of well-being. A new energy seemed to course through every nerve and fiber. Even one of my doctors noticed a change in me.

"Betsy, I don't even know why, but I have the feeling that you are going to recover," he told me, puzzled by this vague "sense."

Eventually I was released from the hospital and I went home, though the chemotherapy treatments continued. Never did I question this as a contradiction of my faith. God is the one who has blessed us with increasing knowledge of medical science. I know that doctors can administer drugs or treatments, but their effectiveness is in the hands of God. And He *is* able to heal independently of doctors and their treatments. Sometimes He does.

As my chemotherapy began, I found that I was being bathed in a different kind of vital treatment—the treatment of prayer.

In the early crisis of my illness, I was really bolstered up with the knowledge that my church family had formed a prayer vigil for me. Your friend may be facing dark sleepless hours as I and my family did. And there are painful, unnerving tests, followed by interminable hours or days of waiting for the results. There is doubt, fear—all the thoughts and emotions I have already described. Yet how comforting to know that every hour of the day or night, a friend is praying for you.

A prayer vigil is simple to arrange.

You may choose to set some time boundaries. Maybe your church or prayer group would feel it best to commit one twenty-four-hour period, a full week or one day each week to intercessory prayer. Then each person chooses a set time— perhaps fifteen, thirty or sixty minutes during that vigil— when they take up the love-burden of prayer for your friend.

One variation on this is the prayer "chain." It can work like a living nervous system, energizing many Christians at once into prayer-action. Again, the plan is simple.

One person may act as the contact between your friend's family or minister. When a crisis arises, the contact calls one other person, who calls another and so on. It is best for everyone to keep a list of names and telephone numbers of all members of the chain in case your contact is not available. In that case, you simply call the next person on the chain. And be sure that everyone is really willing to receive phone calls at odd and late hours if necessary.

As friends, scattered throughout the United States and Europe, heard of my illness, they formed prayer groups to intercede on my behalf. These friends often joined together with Christians I had never met—total strangers. I couldn't comprehend such love, concern and time commitment from friends, let alone strangers. I was often moved to joyful tears at the thought of a love I never knew could exist. How good and comforting and uplifting it felt.

Besides the benefit to me, I sensed that something wonderful was happening for these friends, too.

A letter from one friend touched me, showing how you can begin to identify with a friend who is ill. It said:

Wednesday night at our "Serendipity" session at church, we closed with a circle of prayer. One person could sit in the center of the circle and the others would move in and touch—lay on hands—and pray silently. I felt that the Master Healer wanted me to sit there in your place—and I did. As I felt the warmth of the hands, I prayed that the love would flow through to you.

We were all growing closer to God through my illness. And our faith was stretching into new areas.

Weeks added up to months. My chemotherapy continued through summer, fall and early winter—and so did my prayer "treatments." Chemotherapy often left me exhausted and nauseous. But amazingly, I tolerated it better than most patients, and my white blood cell count did not drop, which could have opened me to other diseases had it done so. I took this as definite evidence of God's presence and protecting touch.

By Christmas, it seemed that the miracle everyone had prayed for was coming to pass. The swelling in my stomach had disappeared. My abdomen was soft and supple again. By June, no apparent symptoms of cancer had existed for several months. Dr. Mozden suggested an exploratory, second-look surgery to check on my progress. And I agreed.

However, the operation revealed that the cancer was not gone. Malignant cells were discovered in five places. They were small enough to fit on the head of a pin—yet they were powder kegs of trouble, carrying enough potential danger to send me back into another year of chemotherapy.

Why didn't God finish the "miracle"? Why did He demonstrate His willingness and ability to heal certain friends and acquaintances, and then allow my cancer to remain? Why did He allow my faith and expectancy to grow? Monty asked the same questions. So did my friends—my faithful prayer partners everywhere.

Later, I was able to ask a different question: What were *God's* plans for me?

I began to search out all the Christian books on healing that I could get my hands on. The authors expressed a gamut of opinions.

At this point in my illness, the first-person accounts of healing left me cold. So did the books that described healing as a "package deal." These seemed to be cut-and-dried: You should be baptized in the Holy Spirit, receive the gift of tongues and then healing would come. I knew this wasn't true because people with only a nominal faith are sometimes healed miraculously as well as the most zealous Christians.

To me these books actually limited God, specifying what He *had* to do in every case, with no variation.

But I did come across other books that avoided the "God-will-do-this-if-you-do-that" formulas. If God has not granted your prayer requests for healing or if the answer is just long in coming, some of these books offer wisdom and comfort.

I heartily agree with the stance taken by Edith Schaeffer in her book *Affliction*. She writes:

"Why don't you pray?" is a question that can be an insult to someone who is already spending sleepless hours in prayer. "If only you had enough faith, everything would change!" is a judgment only God can make. No one can ever know what reality of faith there is present within the person whose prayer does not seem to be answered.

Someone brought me a copy of Agnes Sanford's book *The Healing Light*. I read it eagerly, for I had heard her speak years before at a Young Life staff conference. She had fascinated me. Small of frame, she spoke with such compassion, authority and conviction. Now, in the pages of her book, I learned how to ask God simply to do whatever it was He wanted to do for me. There were no limits and no specifications.

I know that the "let-down" attitude some of my friends displayed added greatly to my own disappointment. When Monty announced that the news of my healing was incorrect, some people accused him, saying he was "just negative." Suddenly I felt that their energy was gone, that they were just tired—tired of praying, tired of waiting for God to work, tired of holding my hand. Devastating waves of loneliness began to wash over me.

Fewer came to my aid now as listeners. It was as if most of my friends could hardly handle their own disappointment without having to hear about mine.

But a few were ready to walk the deeper faith walk with me. One man gave me great encouragement because he was so genuine—and I sensed he was willing to "tough it out" with me. I read and reread these lines from his letter:

Never in my life have I had to contemplate the loss of one I love as much. I know how difficult a time it is for you, and it's a real test of my faith. To me, faith means *not* trying to "understand" things like this. Faith is just knowing God's love is supreme. I thank Him for that confidence. I pray that my confidence will grow through this difficult time.

From these few deeper friendships, I began to learn of a new dimension in prayer.

Every prayer of faith has power, of course, whether it's offered by a church congregation, an informal group or by a solitary person in his own room. While it's vital to pray *for* someone, you can reach a new depth of friendship and faith when you pray *with* them. I don't intend to offer a "formula" for this, but I've come to realize that many Christians still have difficulty with interpersonal prayer—so I'd like to give a few suggestions.

In a quiet room, take hold of your friend's hand while you pray. Something unusual happens when you very gently hold someone's hand in yours. Before the first word is spoken, a tremendous warmth, strength, assurance, affection and faith are imparted. Touch breaks through the natural feelings of isolation and of being forsaken that occur in sickness, and it does so in a way that goes deeper than words.

Look into your friend's eyes, too. We've all seen people avert their eyes from each other in close-up situations—like in a crowded elevator. Most of us have been taught to pray with heads bowed and eyes closed, but it's a custom, not a divine command. I realize this may be a more difficult cultural barrier to hurdle, but a truly wonderful sense of spiritual closeness happens when you pray while looking into a friend's eyes.

Most important, pray simply and specifically. Great "pastoral" prayers that sound lofty but avoid the mundane, personal needs of a friend have a "tinny," unnatural ring to my ear. Is your friend in pain? Or worried about his family, career, upcoming treatments or surgery, finances? Talk with God together in simple language about these specific issues. When you dare to be open and honest in your requests, you may be wonderfully surprised to find that the Holy Spirit has soothed your friend's aching spirit with your own words.

Friends who can walk through an intense, prolonged test of faith seem to be rare. Admittedly, everyone has a different measure of faith. There is no reason to feel guilty; there are still other ways to help your sick friend and his family.

I found another type of love and encouragement coming from my "practical" friends—those who gave themselves sacrificially, helping my family and me in the more mundane struggles of everyday life.

Even if you're not a "prayer warrior," you can still give your friend the gift of service.

7

Helping Hands

The night of my ambulance ride to the hospital, our family faced another real problem besides my medical emergency.

Dimly, I recall my concern for Monty, the girls and our home even through clouds of pain. I had prepared and frozen some meals beforehand, but there were a myriad of practical details we had not prepared to handle. Our dearest friends, those we knew we could count on for help, were thousands of miles away in California. At the hospital, my worries gave way temporarily to the doctor's sedation.

Later, when I woke from surgery, I was tremendously grateful for the practical kind of love that was already flowing toward our family from our brand-new friends in the Northeast.

One man from the church spent his day with Monty in the hospital waiting room during the long operation. They talked in short, quiet spurts or sat in silence. They paced the floor together, eager for news from the surgical team. Since the findings were not good, I was thankful later that Monty had not been alone.

Likewise, Monty's associate pastor, Dennis Doerr, spent the entire afternoon of my operation at our home with Suzanne and Marybeth. He fixed meals and played games, helping to keep their minds off my situation as much as possible.

Finding that my family was being cared for was important to me, of course. Physically, I was in pain, and the diagnosis was emotionally numbing. But at least our practical needs were not adding to my worry bank.

Our families and dear friends around the country would help us in other ways (which I'll describe in the following chapter). But our new friends taught us what it means to help someone who is seriously ill.

What can I do to help? Monty and I have heard that welcome question time after time. Monty often takes people at face value, and in the beginning he would reply, "Well, actually, our house could use a cleaning," or, "You could pick up a load of my shirts and iron them."

Not surprisingly, the person making the offer would sometimes stammer a bit, then let him know that cleaning and ironing weren't exactly what he had in mind. These folks, I suppose, expected Monty to say, "Thanks anyway, but we're just fine. There's nothing you can do for us." Somehow our culture has trained us to give such polite if untrue replies even when we desperately need help.

Not everyone is as open as Monty. Not everyone knows what to expect when they offer to help someone in deep need. It's good to understand some ground rules.

If you plan to make a blanket offer like, "Call me anytime if you need anything," think about it first. If you mean that, fine. Perhaps you might need to be more realistic and honest with yourself and your friend. Put together a list of what you are able to do and the times you are available. Decide whether you are willing to give up personal plans should your friend really take you up on your offer.

Second, be flexible when you can.

One friend called shortly after I returned from the hospital. She wanted to bring a meal. My strength was returning, and I was eager to get reacquainted with my own kitchen. Puttering over the stove made me feel less helpless and more human again.

"Thanks very much," I replied, stirring my kettle of steaming soup. "But I've got things under control for tonight." Then I suggested she plan on another time if possible.

But her ideas were set. "Oh, please let me help you. I've already planned what I'm going to fix." Her frustration boiled over. "People want to help you. You should give them a chance whether you need it or not!"

Another woman called with the offer of a meal. I thanked her for her thoughtfulness also, but again said we were fine in that regard.

Pausing for a moment, she offered a couple of other options and hit on one special area of need. "If you or the children need a ride anywhere, I could do that instead."

This was an offer at which I jumped. Suzanne needed transportation to her weekly guitar lessons, and I was unable to drive.

I soon discovered that this woman's mother had struggled with cancer thirty years earlier. She was sensitive to the innumerable needs a family experiences at such times.

Sensitivity to your friend is another ground rule—and a very important one.

For the first three weeks I was home, there was at least one other person in the house at all times. Including my stay in the hospital, it was six weeks since our family had had dinner and an evening alone.

Just when it looked as though we were going to have a little privacy, I was informed by one family of friends that they were coming by to pick up Suzanne and Marybeth for the afternoon and evening. I knew they meant well; their idea was for Monty and me to have a few quiet hours together. At another time, I would have welcomed that offer. But just then, our family had other needs.

I wanted to spend that time with my girls. They wanted some family time alone, too. They had even marked the calendar with a star on the date when it looked as though we might have a family dinner. We were hoping for a long afternoon of mother-daughter talk, and I wanted so badly to feel the comfort of their sitting beside me on the bed, filling me in on the details of their lives that I was missing.

But no matter how politely or strenuously I refused, these friends were insistent. Plans were already made. They would not take "no" for an answer.

Fortunately, I was able to control the feelings and words that boiled just under the surface. Why were people making decisions for me? How did they know what was "best" for my family? Why couldn't they understand our need to be a family? Or my need to be a mother?

Far more people were very sensitive to our needs. They offered to do what they could, accepted alternative suggestions if necessary and followed through with heartwarming consistency. Basically, they served us in three areas.

There is so much that goes into the upkeep of a home. When someone is ill, there is little time for a family to stay on top of things.

Several men from our church volunteered to maintain the grounds outside our home. They mowed the lawn, pruned bushes and raked. Even on the hottest days of summer, one or more of these men showed up to do yardwork. Monty was freed up to have some extra time with the girls and me.

Indoors, there is plenty of work, too. You might volunteer to clean your friend's home one day a week. Vacuuming, washing floors or windows, cleaning a garage or basement, moving heavy furniture to sweep—these are all things a sick person is incapable of doing, and might not readily ask of a friend.

One group of friends knew we were in the midst of redecorating our new home when I was taken ill. I had started several major projects—only to leave them half-done. True, they weren't uppermost on my mind. But unfinished projects have a way of staring you in the face.

This team of workers checked with me in the hospital. Would I like them to go into the house and finish things off? Did I already have color schemes, fabrics and paint picked out? Should they do it all or leave some for me to finish? Their thoughtful questions hit the spot, not presupposing that I would want everything bright and new when I walked back in the door. It was still my home, and they let me feel that it was.

Sometimes illness may require your friend and his family to travel. Quite often, there is the need to consult with a specialist or take treatments in a hospital or clinic out of town. In this case, your friend may welcome a "house sitter," someone to live in and provide routine upkeep while they are away. Usually, single people are free from other responsibilities and able to serve in this way.

And of course, there are other needs. Laundry has to be done, dishes washed, as well as numerous other functions of daily living that must go on. These border on the second area where you can help your ill friend—that is, with his family.

First of all, be aware that in a crisis, family members need to know they are useful, too. Suzanne and Marybeth are responsible for certain household chores. During our crisis, they went about their normal duties—and some added ones—

aware that they were needed and helpful. Happily, I saw my daughters maturing.

Nevertheless, in spite of these cautionary notes, there are so many ways that concerned friends can help. One woman took on the responsibility of organizing meals. This was valuable during my hospitalizations, and while I was weak and convalescing. Having a single organizer like this is beneficial.

Then there is the need to schedule meals. On certain days or evenings, no one may be home at all. At other times, family from out-of-town may be visiting, in which case the head count for dinner will be higher than usual. On Monday, six o'clock may be fine for dinner—but on Tuesday, the family may need to be out at that time.

A coordinator can also be sure that the meals are varied. Your friends will enjoy the meals even more if they aren't eating chicken six nights in a row.

One final tip in this regard. Beautiful serving dishes are nice and thoughtful, but I was always thankful for meals that came in aluminum and containers that could be thrown away afterward.

If your ill friend is forced into a situation where his or her children are often left alone, your help will be truly welcome. One older couple came to our home every afternoon while I was in the hospital. I was so grateful that the girls did not arrive from school to an empty house.

You may also offer an occasional day at the park or zoo, or a trip to the beach. Opening up your family's recreation time to include other children can teach your child the value of loving and sharing. If needed, you might consider allowing a child to live with your family if the parents have to travel for medical treatments.

Helping with the personal needs of your friend is yet

another way you can be of help.

Often, just knowing there is someone readily available—to help, to listen, to visit—can lift the spirits of the sick person tremendously. The very heart of God is touched when you visit a sick friend, for he identifies with the afflicted. As Jesus said, "I was sick and you looked after me . . . I tell you the truth, whatever you did for one of the least of these brothers of mine, you did for me" (Matthew 25:36, 40).

Again, there are special ground rules to observe in visiting.

Arrange your visit ahead of time. Always make a telephone call to verify your get-together, even if you have scheduled your visit days before. At the last moment your friend may have to decline the planned time together. I was often tired out, or sick from the cancer treatments. Sometimes we were in the midst of an unexpected special family time. I was glad for the friends who followed their inner promptings to call me first, and for their kind understanding when they found that a visit was inappropriate at that time.

As I said in an earlier chapter, you may visit your friend with one idea of how you'd like to fill the time, but leave the "agenda" up to him or her. Needs are often different from what we are hoping to meet.

Depending on your friend's physical limitations, you might suggest a number of ways you can help.

Perhaps your friend is able to get around finally after a long convalescence. You might offer a shopping trip, lunch out or an evening at the theater. The chance to get out of confines will be most welcome, I assure you.

Offer to write letters and answer correspondence as your friend dictates. If your friend is as fortunate about receiving mail as I was, he or she may need this kind of help. Letters seemed to tumble through my bedroom door, mound-

ing up daily like an anthill. I knew that most of these concerned friends who had written were not "expecting" me to
reply, but I wanted so much for them to know about my
condition and how they could pray. You might even bring
notepaper or cards with you for this purpose.

One pastime I enjoyed was having someone read to me. I
was physically able to read to myself much of the time—but it
was so relaxing to hear someone else's voice. And many sick
people are too weak to read to themselves. Earlier, I suggested
some Scripture passages that can encourage the sick. Monty
and I have found several books of special value. (See the list at
the end of this chapter.)

The Last Battle, C.S. Lewis' brilliant conclusion to his *Chron-
icles of Narnia*, has a special place in my heart. Monty often reads
portions of this marvelous little book to other friends who are
seriously ill or facing death. Its effect on me is evidence that
reading it to your friend can do so much more than fill time.

I was hearing the story again one day, having read it to
the girls before. As the book concludes, the main characters
see the land change, wonderfully, mysteriously, before their
eyes. Colors become more true, more beautiful, vibrant and
alive. Trees, rocks and flowers become more "solid" than ever
before. They move ahead, into a glorious new land, "higher
up and further in" to the true Narnia. All at once, they realize
that they have died, passing seamlessly from one life to
another.

As I listened to these fascinating scenes, I was deeply
moved. It was a significant time and a significant passage in
helping me to accept the possibility of my own death.

These are only a few suggestions for reaching out and

helping your friend in practical ways. Undoubtedly, you will discover your own means of serving. Most important, you are giving yourself—and your friend will receive that as a most treasured gift.

Recommended Reading

Getting Well Again, by Carl Simonton
A Touch of Wonder, by Arthur Gordon
Pilgrim's Progress, by John Bunyan
Heaven, by Joseph Bayly
Behold Your God, by Agnes Sanford
Don't Be Afraid to Die, by Gladys Hunt
Till Armegedon, by Billy Graham
A Severe Mercy, by Sheldon Vanauken
Love Is Stronger Than Death, by Peter Kreef

8

Long Distance

Shortly before Jesus' crucifixion, He was eating supper with friends when a woman timidly crept up beside Him. His disciples were puzzled to see her slip from the folds of her cloak a precious alabaster box—her love gift for the Master.

Without a word, she broke open her exquisite treasure. And the exotic fragrance of spikenard—an ointment worth more than one year's wages—flowed out onto Jesus' head.

Impulsive? The disciples thought so, and they complained that it was a waste. Extravagant? Of course. But this woman's love for her Teacher and Friend was worth more to her than her dearest possessions.

I have felt the same kind of extravagant love "pouring" out to me from friends and family who live far away. Within twenty-four hours of my first surgery and shocking prognosis, three friends from California crossed the continent to be at my side. Another West Coast friend came to help when I returned home from the hospital. My sister traveled from out-of-state to help; so did Monty's sister-in-law and parents.

The love they showed involved great sacrifice, and we were overwhelmed. Travel is costly—in money and time. Our friends left families, jobs, churches and personal plans behind; they spent hundreds of dollars. Their extravagance toward me bolstered my sense of self-worth. It gave me the will to fight against death.

In our highly mobile society, it's not unusual for close

friends to live thousands of miles apart. Careers, education and ministries may bring us into close, binding friendships, and then lead us to opposite ends of the country.

Distance does not have to bar you from helping your friend who is ill. Traveling to be at your friend's side is only one way to show your true concern. Telephone calls and correspondence are other ways to show your friend that he is merely out of your sight, and not out of mind and heart.

For those whose finances, family responsibilities and jobs are flexible enough to allow travel, there are some questions you should ask before you call up your travel agent.

First, is this the best time for me to visit? Get in touch with your friend and his family on this one. A number of factors may affect your scheduling.

For example, your friend may be undergoing treatments for his illness, such as I did, that leave him physically uncomfortable. It's hard to appreciate seeing even your dearest friend or favorite relative when you are exhausted or nauseous. Showing up unannounced can be disappointing for both you and your friend if the timing is all wrong.

On the other hand, being there at the right time gives you the chance to help your friend personally in just the right way.

One college friend, whom I hadn't seen in years, phoned to say she was coming to New England for a professional conference. She was eager to see me, even though it meant driving several hundred miles out of her way. The timing was right: I was feeling stronger, and I accepted her kind offer of a visit.

Her stay refreshed me. She hadn't come to "do" anything, just to enjoy our friendship and renew my spirit. Her time was my time. We sat up late at night reminiscing college days, laughing—and crying a little. Days, we went antiquing on the winding, cobbled streets of some North Shore fishing villages. It was exactly what I needed, a chance to "link arms" again with a close friend from my more carefree past.

Another question you need to ask is: Where will I stay?

For any number of reasons, staying in the home of your friend may be inconvenient. During times of illness families seem to need an extra measure of privacy. Too, other out-of-town guests may have scheduled a trip before you. You may need to make arrangements to stay elsewhere or arrange your visit for another time.

A third important question is this: Why am I going?

You might have a specific message of encouragement, a God-given directive to pray a healing prayer, or the desire to serve. Maybe you have a simple, heartfelt urge to be near your friend. These are valid reasons to visit. If you are going out of obligation or guilt, you might better wait until you have another motive. In any case, having a clear purpose in mind can help you be a stabilizing force in a situation where lives have been suddenly interrupted and schedules have become confused.

I still relive the wonderful moments that occurred when those close to my heart but far from my door came to care for me in my illness. The inner strength I gathered from their love is worth much, much more than the money they spent.

If a trip is not possible, perhaps you can set aside a little extra money each week to pay for long-distance telephone visits. Many a long, boring, painful day has been brushed with a fresh coat of joy when I've heard the voice of a friend at the far end of the telephone line. I'm so amazed that a simple phone call can do so much, and now I never ignore those inner nudges of the Spirit to pick up the receiver and reach out to someone in need.

From the calls I've received and those I've placed, I've

learned a few things about telephone visiting.

Many of my callers would start by asking the thoughtful question, "Is this a good time to talk, or would you like me to call back at another time?" They were sensitive, allowing me the chance to decline a conversation when I was with another visitor, if I was sick or tired out from my treatments or in the midst of nursing care. When I couldn't come to the phone, they simply passed along a word of love or encouragement through Monty, one of the girls or whoever happened to answer the phone. Every good wish that came was a new block in the wall of support my friends were building.

If your friend can come to the phone, it's best to get to the purpose of your call immediately. Are you asking for an update on their condition? Are you offering time or help in a specific area of need? Perhaps your message is just, "I love you and I'm praying for you."

It's best not to jabber on and on, launching into a lengthy, one-sided chat. This kind of call is hard to take even when you're feeling well; it's even more wearying and annoying when you are ill. You may recall times when you couldn't get off the phone because your caller would not "come up for air." As a courtesy, you might say at the outset, "If you get tired, please tell me. If I'm in the middle of saying something and you have to interrupt suddenly, I won't mind."

To me, it's most important to convey warm, loving encouragement during a phone visit. Negative emotions like fear, anger or depression might better be expressed at another time in another manner. Your phone call will be more helpful if it serves to settle emotional dust and not stir it up.

This is not to say that emotions and anxieties should be kept hidden. But rather than a burst of emotion on the telephone, it is better to express yourself in a letter—or in many letters if necessary. Some of the letters I have received are read and reread, allowing me to assimilate all that is being said, positive and negative. They minister to me many times over.

The letters Monty and I receive have overwhelmed us by their sheer volume. Each one has touched us in a different way. I would like to share a few brief excerpts and the various ways our friends encouraged us.

> Betsy, thank you for the smile that crinkles the corner of your eyes, for the love you have expressed for so many friends. Thank you for just being Betsy.
>
> Monty, thank you for all the long hours of study and work that have moved you along in serving the Lord.
>
> Lovingly,
> Ed

Ed celebrated our individuality—the things that made us unique to him. I knew he could never write exactly the same note to anyone else he knew.

You can affirm your friend at this difficult time by letting him know what characteristics make him different from your other friends. Take time to think about it: What makes your friend special to you? What are the good qualities that drew you together in the first place?

Anne's letter was strikingly open. To me, it stands as a good example of how to express negative emotions in a constructive way:

> I am afraid and embarrassed. With the problems you are facing, what right do I have to tell you I am afraid? I have found one excuse after another for not coming to see you. With all my heart, I want to reach out and help you and your family. I want to be available and useful.

Most of all, I want to say the words that will make you
well. But the fact remains that I am afraid. I have never
before written anything like this. I hope you will understand and forgive me.

Love,
Anne

I felt privileged that Anne would share with me her true
feelings. I read her letter several times, and I could sympa-
thize with the way her emotions were being torn in two. Had
she blurted out in a telephone conversation something like,
"Betsy, I'm not coming to see you," it would have been harder
to deal with. But her note reminded me again and again that if
I were not her friend, her feelings would not be so knotted up.

One of many letters that renewed a joyful, solid faith in
me came from Patty. In praying for me, certain Scripture lept
into her mind, and as she shared them, they came alive in my
heart, too.

"We know that the one who raised the Lord Jesus
from the dead will also raise us with Jesus and present us
with you in his presence" (II Corinthians 4:14).

That makes me want to say, "Hooray!" It doesn't
matter that I can't come to Boston to see you like the
others have—we'll *all* be together before long in His
presence. How good of Him to tell us!

"Therefore we do not lose heart. Though outwardly
we are wasting away, yet inwardly we are being renewed
day by day. For our light and momentary troubles are
achieving for us an eternal glory that far outweighs
them all. So we fix our eyes not on what is seen, but on
what is unseen. For what is seen is temporary, but what
is unseen is eternal" (II Corinthians 4:16-18).

This sure puts suffering and life and death in perspective, doesn't it?

>I love you, dear sister,
>Patty

Patty was not just preaching or quoting Scripture at me.
We both wanted to see each other again very badly. In that
light, I knew that Paul's words were meaningful to her, and so
they meant even more to me.

Obviously, this Scripture had significance for me and my
illness, too. It reminded me that, for the Christian, eternity is
not something to be feared. We are headed for heaven, where
time and miles will never separate us from our Lord and
dearest friends again.

Another letter reminded me of all the experiences of life
here on earth for which I was thankful. A young woman we
knew during our days in youth ministry wrote these words:

I have such pleasant memories of those days in
Pasadena with you. That Young Life club was the heart
of all our lives . . . That was a long time ago and the stuff
you taught me stuck . . . I remember that little Bible
study we used to have.

A few days ago, I had a flash of that time we all went
to the beach on a bus. On the way home, a bunch of us
sat way in the back and we all had the giggles. Do you
remember that? Every time I think of that I smile.

>Bless you,
>Pat

Memories of all my meaningful relationships flooded
over me as I read Pat's letter. I felt grateful for a full life and
for the privilege of being useful in others' lives.

What is important to note about this letter is the tone. Reminiscing should never become maudlin or overly sentimental. You should never write your friend a letter that says, "Let's go back to those earlier times." That is only fantasy. Pat reminded me of the past, but encouraged with where she was right now in her Christian life.

A girl who had heard of my illness through mutual friends sent a letter that bubbled with hope and possibility:

> I know of your faith, your love, your courage, your strength and warmth . . . I love you, Betsy. I celebrate God's miraculous healing in your life—His power—He knew your faith, He knew He could trust you to be faithful in spite of illness. You must be an extraordinary servant.
>
> Joyfully—lovingly,
> Ann

While she didn't state presumptuously or naively that I *would* be healed, Ann's letter made me say, "Why not? With God, all things are possible." She reminded me of His all-powerful nature without theological heaviness.

These examples are only a dusting from the mountains of mail Monty and I have received. I wish I could share all the cards and letters with you, but these few show a love and compassion and wisdom that can serve as a model for you in your correspondence with a friend who is sick.

I assure you that your thoughtfulness will give your friend a joy that is worth every bit of your effort.

9

My Husband, Monty

Up till now, I've been writing to friends of the sick. And yet my closest, truest friend is my husband, Monty.

No one is more intimately aware of the hardship and turmoil that accompany illness than a husband or wife. Likewise, no one has greater opportunity than a spouse to touch and soothe the deep, inner aches.

Monty and I already had a good, maturing relationship when my cancer was first discovered, because we had spent years ironing out some of the wrinkles in our marriage. But even a good relationship can be strained in the daily battle for life. We know about those struggles from facing the challenge together. Monty's support has been every bit as vital to me as the hours and hours of medical care and treatments—and in many ways, more delicate, painstaking and patient.

I believe Monty's perspective can help those of you whose husband or wife is seriously ill.

Betsy's illness has been a crucible in which every facet of our marriage has been tested with a ferocious heat. When we promised to be faithful to each other "in sickness and in health," we never suspected that vow would actually be tested. Most people don't.

One of the big differences in our relationship after the

onset of Betsy's illness was that everything intensified—our needs, good and bad attitudes, flaws in communications, strengths and weaknesses of character, all showed up with telescopic magnification. And if a weakness shows up, you don't have the luxury of sweeping it under the carpet of a busy home life or career, to be handled later. You are forced to deal with the hard things, and it's worth it.

Generally, I have begun to learn as never before how to be *sensitive, honest* and how to *affirm* my spouse.

The greatest need for sensitivity may come in relation to your partner's self-image. Sickness often brings physical disability. Outward appearance can also change startlingly, especially if your spouse is undergoing certain medical treatments.

When Betsy began chemotherapy, we were warned that, as a side effect, her hair would most likely fall out. Slowly, her dark curly hair began to get thinner, and she expressed her deep anxiety to me and to a few friends. One of these sensitive ladies showed up at our door one day with three boxes. Sitting on the sofa, she removed the lid and displayed three stylish new wigs.

"The store allowed me to bring these samples by for you to try on," our friend explained. "If you like one, I can pay for it when I take the others back."

This simple act helped Betsy to deal with her changing appearance. This woman encouraged her not to hide from the world, but to make the necessary adjustments and keep on moving. Not that the adjustment was easy, as I mistakenly thought.

After years of marriage, I knew where all the lines were drawn—when it was time to be serious or romantic or funny or when it was all right to tease. However, the limits tightened up in some cases, and I found myself needing to redefine certain aspects of our relationship.

For example, Betsy is normally full of fun, able to take a joke better than most people I know. In a light mood one morning, I propped her new wig jauntily on top of my head and began clowning for Suzanne and Marybeth. It was a painful miscalculation.

Betsy was excruciatingly sensitive about our daughters' reaction to having "a mother who's going bald." The wig was an ever-present reminder of her loss. And without ever meaning to, I had trampled across the line into an area where teasing was no longer funny, but hurtful.

Respect your partner's sensitivities. I continue to learn by listening and never assuming, in order to discover where new "lines" have been drawn—what is threatening, what can be openly discussed, what special needs and desires I should be aware of.

Sensitivity goes hand-in-hand with *honesty*. We find it invaluable to set aside a special time that is earmarked for honest, open sharing.

For us, early morning is when we prop ourselves up in bed with pillows—a fresh pot of coffee on the night table—and just talk. Whenever you can manage it, carve out of your day a regular time to talk and listen to your spouse. Comments spoken hastily or in passing are so easily lost *and* misunderstood. For our investment of time, we have a tremendous return in unity—even when it comes to tough issues.

During one of our relaxed moments, Betsy posed a question to me, one that deeply concerned her. She wanted to know how I felt about her—with a huge scar striping her abdomen and with graying, thinning hair.

I paused, sipping my coffee, using that quiet moment to phrase my answer. Knowing Betsy, I realized that she wanted honesty—not flattery—and she wanted assurance.

Looking her in the eyes, I replied, "Honey, I liked you better with hair and without the scar—I'll admit that. But I love you just the same."

Typically, Betsy pursued it further. "Since I've been sick, I know it's been tough for you—sexually, I mean. I guess your physical needs aren't really being fulfilled, are they?"

Again, I faced her head-on openness with honesty. "No, my physical needs haven't been met. But Betsy," I continued with the same honesty, "you know there's more to our marriage than our physical relationship."

Quickly, I listed all those things I loved doing with her. Both of us enjoy exploring the fascinating old villages in the countryside around our new home. Relaxing by the fire is another shared pleasure, and many evenings were spent talking quietly together with soft music in the background. Often, we read books together out loud. And we continue to sleep in the same bed, even during the worst parts of the illness. I assured her that would always continue, no matter what.

Betsy did feel reassured. And I learned two things: Honesty is necessary, and your spouse may resent your hiding or "sugar-coating" the truth; however, strong assurance is equally important.

I found, too, that it's all right to honestly disagree. It's not uncommon for a couple's disagreements to center around the actual fight for life.

During the very tough times, when chemotherapy has made Betsy terribly ill, she's wanted to stop struggling and let the cancer win. Then I've dug in my heels and urged her not to quit. Not unusually, our roles have also reversed. Betsy's desire to fight has sometimes grown strong—just when I'm ready to quit after months of watching the one I love suffer intensely.

You must remember, at such times, that it's your spouse's life and body in question—not yours. No matter how strong our disagreement, I have always assured Betsy that I am behind her 100 percent whether she decides to continue fighting the illness or give in.

People often try to duck another issue when straight honesty would be much better. Someone who is seriously ill may need to talk about death—not in an abstract way, but *his own death*. This is not hysteria or melancholy; it's a true psychological, spiritual and emotional need. We perform a terrible disservice—to anyone we love deeply—by patting them on the hand and saying, "Oh, don't talk about dying—you're not going to die."

Once when Betsy's illness took a turn for the worse, I noticed an unusual, faraway look in her eyes, sensed a deep inner calm and knew she wanted to talk. From previous remarks, I realized she often thought about death, and even her own memorial service—and I suspected those thoughts were again on her mind.

"Betsy," I said gently, perching on the foot of her bed, "have you thought about the kind of funeral you'd like? I really want to know what your wishes are."

Yes, she had definite wishes—no funeral, but a "celebration of resurrection" after burial, and she'd chosen favorite hymns and certain comforting Scriptures, too. It was a healthy release—not at all morbid—as Betsy talked about the possibility of dying.

We talk about other sensitive subjects, too, whenever either of us feels the need. For Betsy, the rearing of our girls is a huge concern, of course. Some parents naturally have a hard time "letting go" of their children. Consider how hard it would be if there was a chance you wouldn't be around to help them grow up. Like every other loving parent, Betsy has hopes and dreams for our girls. Sharing these with me helps to ease the pain of thinking she might not see these hopes to fruition herself.

Talking about the girls occasionally leads Betsy to talk of my remarriage, should she die. The first time she expressed this wish, I immediately and automatically said that remarriage was the farthest thought from my mind. Far from being reassured by my commitment of love, she was a little dismayed.

"Monty," she returned, "the greatest compliment to our marriage would be your desire to be happily married again. And I want the girls to enjoy a mother's love."

You, too, can learn to dignify your spouse's wishes by listening and not simply cutting him off out of fear or embarrassment.

Another act of love is *affirming* your spouse by a commitment to deepening your marriage relationship, and by encouraging the other to reach personal goals.

As much as possible, we try to take the focus off Betsy's illness. We can't deny or escape its reality, nor do we try. But if we're not careful, we may miss precious hours of love, happy experiences and accomplishments by allowing sickness to dominate every waking thought. For us, life is too great a gift to let one day be wasted on self-pity.

Some couples mistakenly "throw in the towel" when it comes to building their relationship. Never is a strong marriage commitment more crucial than when illness strikes.

I've already mentioned our morning conversations over coffee, drives in the country and evenings by the fire. We also attended a "Marriage Encounter" retreat—a weekend of interaction designed, as their literature says, to help make a good marriage better. We were encouraged to talk about strengths and weaknesses we saw in each other, and to renew our commitment of love. We came away with a fresh desire to mature together. For couples who normally have a difficult time expressing their deepest feelings, there are many good seminars like this that can help.

Too, we all have goals and dreams. Betsy has always been my best critic and best advocate in building my ministry. Now I encourage her, too, in fulfilling specific, attainable goals—like writing. Investing in a portable electric typewriter has brought to reality Betsy's goal of writing a book to help others.

In all these things, we can affirm the value of life, of close relationships, of meaningful dreams that God has embedded in our hearts.

Although this chapter is mainly written about husband-wife relationships, I want to say a word about support from outside your marriage. Some couples think they shouldn't "burden" others with their problems, when the love and strength of friends is most needed.

For the first two years of Betsy's illness, we met each week with a support group of eight people. They allowed us to share our honest feelings—our happy moments and our defeats—and they prayed through our crises along with us. These warm, supportive friends gave us an extra boost at the many points when our ability to cope with the illness or to trust in God was weakened.

If you or your spouse are not comfortable opening your sensitive feelings to a group, let me recommend that you find a close friend with whom you can talk honestly.

In short, be in touch with your feelings. Allow yourself the right to feel hurt or angry or lonely or depressed. I'm very aware of the desire to "be strong" for the sake of your spouse. But I also know the value of having a friend to rely on when I need a sounding board before sharing my thoughts and feelings with Betsy.

I have gone through intense agony during Betsy's illness, but out of it has come a deeper love for my wife and a total respect for her courage. In fact, Betsy's tenacity of spirit has not only helped all who know her to grow spiritually, but has also been transferred to the pages of this book.

10

When the Road Gets Long

Dr. Mozden's receptionist greeted me like an old friend, and motioned me toward a seat in the waiting room. I settled near the window. The room was quiet except for the hum of an air conditioner—a welcome relief from the sultry June sun in which I'd been driving.

The number of times I'd consulted with Dr. Mozden were beyond counting. My first treatments were followed by second-look surgery, which had revealed several microscopic spots of persistent cancer cells. Twelve months of more chemotherapy followed.

During the therapy, I'd remained quite healthy. In the fall, I'd begun writing, encouraged by Monty. Even the long winter didn't slow me down. I ice-skated, did some cross-country skiing and joined in a few neighborhood games of hockey on the Charles River. In the spring, I was put on milder drugs and I believed things were looking up.

Now I was eager to discontinue chemotherapy completely. I was concerned about the effects these toxic drugs were having upon my vital organs—my heart, kidneys, liver. It wasn't worth it, I told myself, to nip the cancer and maim or kill me anyway with chemotherapy.

"Betsy," the receptionist was beckoning me, "Dr. Mozden will see you now." I rose and followed her, half-expecting what my trusted friend was about to suggest.

"I recommend another full year of chemotherapy treatments, Betsy." Dr. Mozden was warm but businesslike as usual.

"Doctor," I began, patient but firm, "after two years of chemotherapy, I'm not at all sure I can stand any more. Don't you think those microscopic trouble spots are eradicated by now?"

With great understanding and patience, Dr. Mozden reminded me of the insidious nature of ovarian cancer—and the danger of its recurrence.

Still I persisted. I had months of prayer and good health behind me—and I'd come to believe I was healed. I wanted to close this chapter, and get on with my life.

"You told me that we may need third-look surgery. As much as I hate the thought, I'd like to go ahead with it now. I'd rather know what we're dealing with and be done with it."

Somewhat reluctant, he agreed, and scheduled the surgery.

In the operating room I chatted confidently with the surgical staff. Dr. Mozden smiled and squeezed my hand just as the room began to turn before my eyes.

"I don't think we'll find anything . . ."

When I woke, Monty was beside me, silently stroking my forehead. I'd expected the surgical staff to greet me in the recovery room with triumphant grins. Monty's look of pain told me everything.

"They found two dime-shaped growths. Both malignant."

My head fell back on the pillow. Tears slid out of the corners of my eyes.

Monty continued—softly, directly. "Betsy, Dr. Mozden says more therapy *might* help—but there's no guarantee. Of course, the decision to fight is yours. That's a big part of the battle."

Fight! What does everyone think I've been doing? I only shook my head, unable to speak because of the lump in my throat.

After all the praying, all of the internal fighting, we were no further ahead than when we'd started—months and months and months ago. The questions came in a torrent: What was God up to? What was His plan for me? I knew He was capable of a complete cure; why did He withhold it from me?

I wish I could write a convincing, direct-from-God answer to those questions, so that all of you who have been praying for a sick friend would be satisfied. But again, I come back to the apostle Paul, a fellow sufferer, who asked three times that the "thorn" be removed from his flesh. Now I can receive God's answer, too: "My grace is sufficient for you."

While I was working through my own letdown, I wanted friends to surround me more than ever—to walk the path with me through hurt and despair. I knew they must be tired of praying, hoping, encouraging, keeping a smile on their faces while visiting me. But I was sure they would rally around us and help carry my emotional burden again.

My hopes were nearly shattered.

To be sure, there was no letup in cards, letters, people to clean house or carry in meals—and I was thankful for this kind of continued help. What changed—dramatically—was the attitude. Some hurried in and out with hardly a word spoken. Few asked about the surgery, and fewer wanted to know how I felt inside. I could hardly blame anyone, but I felt abandoned on a dark, drifting slab of emotions.

But I wasn't abandoned totally.

A few weeks after my third-look surgery I was back in the hospital, undergoing tests to see if my body could withstand more chemotherapy. Angry, tired and confused, I was ready to forget the tests and have Monty take me home. I simply wanted to quit.

I was staring up at the dead-white, sterile ceiling when my friend Gretchen came in. I was miserable company—barely looking at her, no smile. And when she told me how sorry she was about the recent findings, I let loose a flood of tears and hurts—all of which she'd been through before.

She listened till I was through, then tried to comfort me. I was so depressed I almost missed what she was saying. After all, I didn't even want to be with me anymore, so why should she?

After our short visit, she rose to leave. Gently, she took my hand in hers. With that winsome, loving look in her eyes, she assured me, "Betsy, I'll always be here if you need me. Just let me know what I can do."

I watched her slip out through the door, and suddenly I heard another message in the words she'd spoken. A small voice was ringing in my ears, speaking directly to my heart. It said: *Fight it, Betsy! Don't give up. You have friends who will stick it out with you—because you're worth fighting for!*

Bodily I struggled and, gripping the side rail, sat up in bed. Floods of courage surged through me like fresh new life inside. I even felt physically stronger.

"I *will* take more chemotherapy. I'll fight it!" Once again my spirit was renewed, soaring in the love of friends who cared enough to stand with me in the toughest times.

It is a rare friend who will draw close when the road gets long and rough. Perhaps your friend has been suffering for a long, long time with no end of illness in sight. Or perhaps the end is clear and it's only a matter of weeks or months. If you are willing to walk the long road, I want to encourage you with another passage of Scripture written by the apostle Paul.

Love suffers long and is kind . . . Love bears all things, believes all things, hopes all things, endures all things. Love never fails . . . And now abide faith, hope and love, these three; but the greatest of these is love.
(I Corinthians 13:4, 7, 8, 13, NKJV)

Paul speaks to me about a durable, steadfast love—not a feeling that is blown away by tough times, bad news or inconvenience. No doubt this kind of strong love was rare in Paul's day, as it seems to be now. Sometimes we just get too busy with our fast-paced lives to stick it out, so we leave caring in the hands of nurses, doctors, nursing home staffs— the paid professionals. Their responsibility is only medical— ours is spiritual.

By now, you may have discovered the love gift you are best equipped to give to your friend. Paul's words remind me that I'm not fulfilling a one-time obligation or laying out one impressive pile of gifts, like Christmas morning. The best gift I can give is to draw in close and stay there.

Are you able to send encouraging cards and letters? Make it a regular habit. Are you willing to continue faithfully in prayer? Don't ever stop. Tell your friend how you are praying, and any encouragement you receive personally. I have been stunned and elated many times when I've been praying alone at home for a specific need of a friend, only to find that they have been blessed with the answer at the same moment. If you are a gifted helper, one who is cheerful at cooking, cleaning, babysitting, running errands, remember that no act of kindness is ever wasted, nor is it forgotten by God.

When I am the one in a position to help a friend and it seems like a long, hard, uphill road, I remind myself of Paul's words in another New Testament letter:

Let us not become weary in doing good, for at the proper time we will reap a harvest if we do not give up
(Galatians 6:9).

Epilogue

Betsy's third-look surgery was followed by three more aggressive rounds of chemotherapy, after which she made the brave decision to stop treatments. While Dr. Mozden counseled her to continue, he yielded to her wishes. Both knew they were on uncharted seas; no decision was absolutely right or wrong.

She returned full-stride to a normal life, and continued writing this book. Her only complaint was an increasingly sore and tender back. Once, while cross-country skiing at Killington, Vermont, she took a final spill. Pain stabbed through her back and tears began to boil. What frustration she felt, cutting short that lovely March day in the snow with the Green Mountains standing so majestically in the sunshine and cold New England air.

Two months later, a battery of tests at University Hospital showed that the disease had spread from its original site. Cancer cells were found in her liver, pelvic bone and a vertebra of the lower back. Once again, aggressive chemotherapy was applied. But in November 1981, the toxicity of the drugs and the spreading cancer proved to be too great, and treatments stopped.

The Hospice of the Good Shepherd was called into service when Betsy came home from the hospital for the last time on January 2, 1982. A hospital bed was moved into our master bedroom along with oxygen tanks—for the disease had attacked her right lung cavity. Round-the-clock nursing care began, and pain medications were needed more and more frequently.

Betsy's goal was to spend her last days at home, as comfortably as possible. At times, she seemed to be taking care of unfinished business.

One chilly evening, as I sat beside her on the bed, Betsy surprised me with a set of simple requests. "Would you mind lighting a fire in the fireplace?" she asked, squeezing my hand weakly. "I'd like to have tea together—by candlelight."

Downstairs, I quickly laid a fire, set the kettle on the stove to boil and lit two slender candles. I hurried back up to her room. Lifting Betsy's frail form in my arms, I carried her gently, like a bride, down to the family room. Before the fireplace, we sat sipping our tea, talking or quietly listening to the pop and sizzle of flaming logs. In the candles' glow, we enjoyed a happy, aimless conversation for nearly an hour, until Betsy's thin shoulders sagged with exhaustion.

Then I carried her back upstairs. She never got out of the bed again.

A few days later, it was clear that our hours together—our minutes—were fast slipping away. Betsy lay struggling for air on the broken line between consciousness and coma—between this world and the next. In one of her lucid moments, with the hiss of oxygen in our ears, we leaned our heads together.

"Honey," I whispered, "it won't be long before we'll all be together again—you, me, Suzanne and Marybeth."

Faintly, she nodded, her eyes drifting into that far-off gaze.

"I hope you'll be waiting at the door for us when we come home." There wasn't time to say more; Betsy's eyes were closed.

On the evening of January 15, 1982, Betsy experienced God's ultimate healing. She is at home now with Him—and we await a joyful reunion.

Monty Burnham
West Newton,
Massachusetts.